MW00618789

America, a Christian Nation?

Examining the Evidence of the Christian Foundation of America

Stephen McDowell

PROVIDENCE FOUNDATION
CHARLOTTESVILLE, VIRGINIA

America, a Christian Nation?
Examining the Evidence of the Christian Foundation of America
By Stephen McDowell

Copyright © 2004 by Stephen McDowell
First printing, 2005
Second printing, 2009

Published by:
Providence Foundation
PO Box 6759
Charlottesville, VA 22906
434-978-4535
Email: info@providencefoundation.com
www.providencefoundation.com

The Providence Foundation is a Christian educational organization whose purpose is to train and network leaders of education, business, and politics to transform their culture for Christ.

Cover pictures: Large painting — Baptism of Pocahontas at Jamestown, Virginia, 1613, by John G. Chapman, courtesy Architect of the Capitol. Smaller panels, from left to right — portion of the First Prayer in Congress, September 7, 1774, courtesy of WallBuilders; National Motto on American money; portion of The Embarkation of the Pilgrims, a print from the original painting in the U.S. Capitol; National Motto above Speaker's Rostrum in U.S. House of Representatives, Capitol Building; portion of Washington's oath of office with his hand on the Bible at his inauguration, April 30, 1789, Currier & Ives print.

Printed in the United States of America

ISBN-10: 1-887456-18-X
ISBN-13: 978-1-887456-18-0

America, a Christian Nation?

Examining the Evidence of the Christian Foundation of America

Periodically, a public person will refer to America as a Christian nation. This usually produces strong responses. When the governor of Mississippi referred to America as a Christian nation a few years ago, many in the media and academia responded in an apoplectic rage to what they consider an idea only recently propagated by "right-wing" Christian revisionist historians. They say America is not now, nor ever has been, a Christian nation.

Is America a Christian nation? Was America ever a Christian nation? Is there such a thing as a Christian nation? The answer to these questions depends upon how you define "Christian nation." As defined below, yes, there is such a thing as a Christian nation, America began as a Christian nation, and today we are in some sense still a Christian nation, but have been progressively moving away from our Christian roots while embracing humanistic ideas. To more fully understand these answers, let us define *Christian nation*.

Definition of a Christian nation

To define a Christian nation, we must first state what it is not. A *Christian nation* is not one where Christianity is the established religion, nor one where every citizen is a Christian, nor one where a majority of the citizens are Christian. It is also not a nation that is without sin, for all men and nations have sinned.

During the time of American colonization, Europe had state established religion — state churches. Many who came to America fled the negative effects of such an establishment, though most of the early colonies had an establishment of religion. At Independence, 8 of the 13 colonies had a specific denomination as the established religion, and 4 others had general Protestant Christianity receiving preference. The national government under the United States Consti-

Washington taking the Presidential oath of office with his hand on the Bible.

tution had no such establishment. State establishments were gradually ended due to the advancement of Christian ideas of religious liberty; yet, Christianity remained "the great vital element" in our nation. If a Christian nation is one defined where Christianity is the established religion, then, on a national level, America was not a Christian nation.

The Senate Committee on the Judiciary in 1853 defined the first amendment clause, "an establishment of religion," as: "It was the connection, with the state, of a particular religious society, by its endowment at the public expense, in exclusion of, or in preference to, any other, by giving to its members exclusive political rights, and by compelling the attendance of those who rejected its communion upon its worship or religious observance."[1] As defined this way, America had no establishment of religion.

If the definition of a Christian nation is one where every citizen is a Christian, then we were not a Christian nation, for all were not Christians (though 99% of early Americans embraced the Christian religion, at least verbally and culturally). Similarly, not all our leaders were Christian, even though laws in several states had this as a qualification for serving in government.

Some might define a Christian nation as one where a majority of the citizens are Christian. While this could have been the situation in early America (a vast majority claimed to be Christian, though God knows the heart), this is not an appropriate measurement of what should constitute a Christian nation.

So were we ever a Christian nation? The Founders certainly spoke of America as a Christian nation. Consider just a few quotes.

John Jay, first Supreme Court Chief Justice, proclaimed, "Providence has given to our people the choice of their rulers, and it is the duty, as well as the privilege and interest of our Christian nation, to select and prefer Christians for their rulers."[2]

John Jay

Chief Justice John Marshall stated:

> The American population is entirely Christian, & with us, Christianity & Religion are identified. It would be strange, indeed, if with such a people, our institutions did not presuppose Christianity, & did not often refer to it, & exhibit relations with it.[3]

The Legislature of New York declared in 1838:

> This is a Christian nation. Ninety-nine hundredths, if not a larger proportion, of our whole population, believe in the general doctrines of the Christian religion.[4]

John Marshall

In *Church of the Holy Trinity v. United States* (1892), the U.S. Supreme Court said "this is a Christian nation" and presented much historical evidence in support of this declaration.[5]

In the view of our Founders, having many citizens personally embrace Christianity is an important part of a Christian nation, but a Christian nation is more than this. A Christian nation is a nation that is founded upon Biblical principles, where Biblical truth and law are the standard for public life, law, and societal institutions. Defined this way, America certainly was a Christian nation, and in some sense still is, as the vestiges of these Christian principles still support aspects of the American society, though they have been progressively undermined during the last century or so.

Every nation is established upon some set of principles or presuppositions, which ultimately is rooted in the faith of the people. Thus all nations have a religious foundation. America was founded upon the principles of Christianity and, therefore in this sense, was a Christian nation. Let's examine some of the evidence.

Evidence of America founded as a Christian nation

Many have argued today against the idea that America was a Christian nation. Arguments have come from non-Christians, such as in the book *Our Godless Constitution*, as well as Christians (some pointing to early sins such as slavery, some to a lack of explicit declaration in the Constitution, others saying Masons were a predominant secret influence and hence we were not Christian). America was not an ecclesiastic nation (where the church ruled), nor one that had no sin, but Christianity was the unofficial religion of early America. The Bible was the foundation of our republic. We were founded on the precepts of Christianity as a Christian nation. The evidence of this Christian foundation is broad.

1. The motive and Christian influence in colonization

Quoting from just a few of the early charters shows the Christian motives for founding the colonies and the recognition of God as the highest authority and source of law:

- First Charter of Virginia (1606): The third paragraph of the charter speaks of their desire to propagate the "Christian Religion to such People, as yet live in Darkness and miserable Ignorance of the true Knowledge and Worship of God, and in time bring the Infidels and Savages, living in those parts, to human Civility, and to a settled and quiet Government."[6]
- The Mayflower Compact was written by a small group of English separatists seeking religious and civil freedom, who were

undertaking the planting of a colony "for the Glory of God, and Advancement of the Christian Faith."[7]

Seal of Rhode Island

- Adopted January 14, 1639, the Fundamental Orders of Connecticut began with the inhabitants covenanting together under God "to maintain and preserve the liberty and purity of the gospel of our Lord Jesus which we now profess." It gave the governor and magistrates "power to administer justice according to the Laws here established, and for want thereof according to the rule of the word of God."[8]

- The Charter of Maryland (1632) revealed the motive of Catholic proprietor Cecil Calvert, Lord Baltimore, in establishing the colony of Maryland — "being animated with a laudable, and pious Zeal for extending the Christian religion."[9]

The Mayflower Compact as written by William Bradford in *Of Plymouth Plantation*.

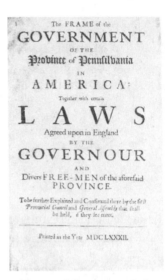

The FRAME of the
GOVERNMENT
OF THE
Province of Pennsilvania
IN
A M E R I C A:
Together with certain
L A W S
Agreed upon in England
BY THE
GOVERNOUR
AND
Divers F R E E - M E N of the aforesaid
P R O V I N C E.
To be further Explained and Confirmed there by the first
Provincial Council and *General Assembly* that shall
be held, if they see meet.

Printed in the Year M.DC.LXXXII.

Frame of Government of
Pennsylvania

- Charter of Rhode Island (1663) — The charter mentioned their intentions of "godlie edifieing themselves, and one another, in the holie Christian ffaith and worshipp" and their desire for the "conversione of the poore ignorant Indian natives."[10]
- The Salem Covenant of 1629: "We Covenant with the Lord and one with an other; and doe bynd our selves in the presence of God, to walke together in all his waies, according as he is pleased to reveale himselfe unto us in his Blessed word of truth."[11]
- Frame of Government of Pennsylvania (1682): The Preamble begins: "When the great and wise God had made the world, of all his creatures, it pleased him to chuse man his Deputy to rule it: and to fit him for so great a charge and trust, he did not only qualify him with skill and power, but with integrity to use them justly."[12]
- Section one of the Pennsylvania Charter of Privileges (1701) contains qualifications of officers where "all Persons who

The Pilgrims observed a day of prayer and fasting before leaving for the new world. They covenanted together under God to form a civil body politic.

also profess to believe in Jesus Christ, the Saviour of the World, shall be capable (notwithstanding their other Persuasions and Practices in Point of Conscience and Religion) to serve this Government in any Capacity, both legislatively and executively."[13]

Covenant nature of documents

In the *Colonial Origins of the American Constitution*, Donald Lutz includes 80 foundational civil documents written in the American colonies. Even a brief examination of these confirms that all 13 colonies embraced a Biblical view of law. In his outline of "some of the things that a reading of these documents together leads us to conclude," Lutz gives number one as: "Political covenants were derived in form and content from religious covenants used to found religious communities." He writes that one element of a political covenant is "an oath calling on God as a witness or partner."[14]

2. The foundation and source of our law was Christian.

Americans had a Christian view of law; that is, God and the Bible were the source of law for America. This is attested to in their own writings, as well as in the writings of those political writers who shaped their thinking.

Dr. Donald Lutz conducted an exhaustive ten-year research of about 15,000 political documents of the Founders' Era (1760–1805), and, from 916 of these items, recorded every reference our Founders made to other sources. This list of 3154 citations reveals

William Blackstone

those writings and men that most shaped the political ideas of our Founders. By far, the most quoted source of their political ideas was the Bible, 34% of citations. The next most quoted sources were individuals who had a Christian view of law — Montesquieu (8.3%), Blackstone (7.9%), and Locke (2.9%).[15]

When the Founders wrote of "the laws of nature and of nature's God" they understood this to mean what Locke, Blackstone,

Montesquieu and others had presented; i.e. "the laws of nature" is the will of God revealed in creation and the conscience of man, and "the laws of nature's God" is the will of God revealed in the Scriptures.

The Words of the Founders

To substantiate that the Founders held a Christian view of law, consider the following statements.

James Otis, an early leader in the struggle for independence, presented the colonists' view of the laws of nature in his famous pamphlet "The Rights of the British Colonies Asserted and Proved:"

To say the Parliament is absolute and arbitrary is a contradiction. The Parliament cannot make 2 and 2, 5: Omnipotency cannot do it. The supreme power in a state . . . strictly speaking, belongs alone to God. Parliaments are in all cases to declare what is for the good of the whole; but it is not the declaration of Parliament that makes it so: There must be in every instance a higher authority, viz. God. Should an Act of Parliament be against any of His natural laws, which are immutably true, their declaration would be contrary to eternal truth, equity, and justice, and consequently void.[16]

Samuel Adams, Signer of the Declaration and Father of the American Revolution: "In the supposed state of nature, all men are equally bound by the laws of nature, or to speak more properly, the laws of the Creator."[17]

John Jay, first Chief Justice of the U.S. Supreme Court: "[T]he . . . natural law was given by the Sovereign of the Universe to all mankind."[18]

James Wilson (1742-1798), signer of the Declaration and the Constitution, U.S. Supreme Court Justice (1789-1798, appointed by Washington); professor of law at Philadelphia College (1790 ff), pub-

Samuel Adams

lished with Thomas McKean, *Commentaries on the Constitution of the United States* (1792):

> God . . . is the promulgator as well as the author of natural law.[19]

> All [laws], however, may be arranged in two different classes. 1) Divine. 2) Human. . . . But it should always be remembered that this law, natural or revealed, made for men or for nations, flows from the same Divine source: it is the law of God. . . . Human law must rest its authority ultimately upon the authority of that law which is Divine.[20]

John Quincy Adams, sixth President: "[T]he laws of nature and of nature's God . . . of course presupposes the existence of a God, the moral ruler of the universe, and a rule of right and wrong, of just and unjust, binding upon man, preceding all institutions of human society and of government."[21]

Alexander Hamilton

Alexander Hamilton, quoting Blackstone: "[T]he law of nature, 'which, being coeval with mankind and dictated by God himself, is, of course, superior in obligation to any other. It is binding over all the globe, in all countries, and at all times. No human laws are of any validity, if contrary to this.'" [22]

Noah Webster, in his definition of *law*: The " 'Law of nature' is a rule of conduct arising out of the natural relations of human beings established by the Creator and existing prior to any positive precept [human law]. . . . These . . . have been established by the Creator and are, with a peculiar felicity of expression, denominated in Scripture, 'ordinances of heaven.'"[23]

Rufus King, signer of the Constitution: "[T]he . . . law established by the Creator . . . extends over the whole globe, is everywhere and at all times binding upon mankind. . . . [This] is the law of God by which he makes his way known to man and is paramount to all human control." [24]

William Findley, U.S. Congress, Revolutionary soldier: "The law of nature being coeval with mankind and dictated by God Himself is of course superior to [and] the foundation of all other laws."[25]

In Federalist 43, **James Madison** responds to the question, On what principle can the federation be superseded without the unanimous consent of the parties to it? (asked in 43.29), by replying: "The first question is answered at once by recurring to the absolute necessity of the case; to the great principle of self-preservation; to the transcendent law of nature and of nature's God." (43.30)[26]

James Madison

Jefferson is less explicit in stating his belief in the origin of law, but he was clear in his belief that rights do not originate from rulers or from man but from God and the universal law of nature: "The God who gave us life gave us liberty at the same time."[27] In the Declaration he speaks of "the laws of nature and of nature's God" and "that all men . . . are endowed by their Creator with certain unalienable rights."[28]

The first Americans to write law commentaries presented this same viewpoint. **Zephaniah Swift** (1759-1823), lawyer, congressman, judge, Chief Justice of the Connecticut Supreme Court (1806-19), assisted in revising the laws of Connecticut and wrote the first law commentary in 1795-96 (*A System of the Laws of the State of Connecticut*), in which he stated:

> [T]he transcendent excellence and boundless power of the Supreme Deity . . . [has] impressed upon them those general and immutable laws that will regulate their operation through the endless ages of eternity. . . . These general laws . . . are denominated the laws of nature.[29]

Thomas Jefferson

James Kent's *Commentaries on American Law* (1826-30) served as the standard general treatise on law in the United States for many decades. Kent wrote in his commentaries:

> Vattel . . . and all the other great masters of ethical and national jurisprudence, place the foundation of the law of nature in the will of God, discoverable by right reason, and aided by Divine revelation. . . .
>
> The law of nature, by the obligations of which individuals and states are bound, is identical with the will of God, and that will is ascertained. . . either by consulting Divine revelation, where that is declamatory, or by the application of human reason where revelation is silent.[30]

Kent agreed with the "masters of jurisprudence" that law is rooted in Divine revelation. Joseph Story, Supreme Court Justice and author of a commentary on the Constitution, presents the same ideas in some of his writings.

Textbooks in schools also presented the view that law is rooted in Divine revelation. **Andrew Young**'s *First Lessons in Civil Government* (1846) states:

> The will of the Creator is the law of nature which men are bound to obey. But mankind in their present imperfect state are not capable of discovering in all cases what the law of nature requires; it has therefore pleased Divine Providence to reveal his will to mankind, to instruct them in their duties to himself and to each other. This will is revealed in the Holy Scriptures, and is called the law of revelation, or the Divine law.[31]

creases its own.

§ 16. But it may be asked, if the law of nature is the rule by which mankind ought to regulate their conduct, of what use are written laws? The will of the Creator is the law of nature which men are bound to obey. But mankind in their present imperfect state are not capable of discovering in all cases what the law of nature requires; it has therefore pleased Divine Providence to reveal his will to mankind, to instruct them in their duties to himself and to each other. This will is revealed in the Holy Scriptures, and is called the law of revelation, or the Divine law.

Young's Textbook, *First Lessons in Civil Government* (1846)

There were those Americans who who did not have this Christian view of law, for example Thomas Paine. In the *Declaration of Rights* (1794, from prison in France) Paine wrote "the Law . . . is the expression of the general will. . . . [T]he rights of man rests on the national sovereignty. This sovereignty . . . resides essentially in the whole people."[32] Paine's ideas on law, as well as his anti-Christian views, were not well accepted in America.[33]

3. The nature and content of specific laws

Early laws written by the Colonists before America's Independence reveal that they looked to the Bible for the source of their laws and the ordering of civil society. A few examples follow:

- "Laws Divine, Morall, and Martiall, etc." written in Virginia between, 1609-1612 — The colonists were required to serve God, to attend divine services, to not speak against God or blaspheme God's holy name, and to not speak or act in any way that would "tend to the derision, or despight [open defiance] of Gods holy word upon paine of death."[34]

- Laws of the Pilgrims (1636, revised 1658, 1671, 1685) — The preface to the 1671 *Book of Laws* states that "Laws . . . are so far good and wholesome, as by how much they are derived from, and agreeable to the ancient Platform of Gods Law."[35] The specific statutes reflected their Biblical philosophy of life. They even quoted Scriptures to support many of their Capital Laws.

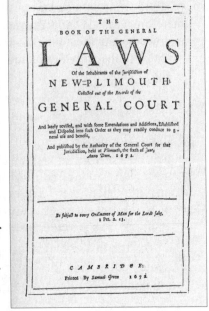

- Massachusetts Body of Liberties (1641) — Section 1 states that no man's life or property can be taken except by some express law that has been sufficiently published, "or in case of the defect of a law in any parteculer case by the word of god."[36]

- What became known as *The Blue Laws of Connecticut* acknowledged "that the supreme power of making laws, and of repealing them, belong to God only, and that by him, this power is given to Jesus Christ, as Mediator, Math. 28:19. Joh. 5:22. And that the Laws for holinesse, and Righteousness, are already made, and given us in the scriptures."[37]

- The Frame of Government of Pennsylvania recognized the Lord's Day (the Sabbath), Biblical standards for marriage — "all marriages (not forbidden by the law of God, as to nearness of blood and affinity by marriage) shall be encouraged,"— and Biblical qualifications for civil officials — "all . . . shall be such as possess faith in Jesus Christ."[38] All offenses against God were to be discouraged and punished, and many were listed. Religious freedom was granted to all persons "who confess and acknowledge the one Almighty and eternal God, to be the Creator, Upholder and Ruler of the world."[39]

William Penn, the author of the Frame of Government of Pennsylvania

Documents in the early American Republic also reveal our Christian foundations. After Independence the State Constitutions acknowledged God as the Supreme Power and provided for the protection of God-given inalienable rights of man. Most required elected officials to take a Christian oath of office, thus subordinating themselves to the highest authority of God.

- The Declaration of Independence, 1776: "the laws of nature and of nature's God"; "all men are created equal, that they are endowed by their Creator with certain unalienable Rights"; "appealing to the Supreme Judge of the world for the rectitude of our intentions"; "with a firm reliance on the Protection of Divine Providence"

- The Constitution of Maryland (1776) states: "it is the duty of every man to worship God in such manner as he thinks most acceptable to him; all persons, professing the Christian religion, are equally entitled to protection in their religious liberty." The oath of office included "a declaration of a belief in the Christian religion."[40]

- The Constitution of Massachusetts (1780) acknowledged "the goodness of the great Legislator of the universe . . . His providence. . . . and devoutly imploring His direction." It declared: "It is the right as well as the duty of all men in society, publicly, and at stated seasons, to worship the SUPREME BEING, the great Creator and Preserver of the universe." It also recognized that "the happiness of a people, and the good order and preservation of civil government, essentially depend upon piety, religion, and morality."[41]

- The Constitution of New Hampshire (1784) recognized "morality and piety, rightly grounded on evangelical

previously formed.
Article the Third. Religion, morality and knowledge, being neceſſary to good government and the happineſs of mankind, fchools and the means of education ſhall forever be encouraged. The utmoſt good faith ſhall always be obſerved towards the Indians; their lands and property ſhall never be taken from them without their conſent; and in their property, rights and liberty, they never ſhall be invaded or diſturbed, unleſs in juſt and lawful wars authoriſed by Congreſs; but laws founded in juſtice and humanity ſhall from time to time be made, for preventing wrongs being done to them; and for preſerving peace and friendſhip with them.

The Northwest Ordinance declared that schools should teach religion, morality, and knowledge because these are the foundations of good government and happiness in civil society.

The Constitution requires a Christian oath, acknowledges the Christian Sabbath, and is dated in the year of our Lord.

principles" as the "best and greatest security to government."[42]

- The Constitution of South Carolina (1776): "The qualifications of electors shall be that [he] . . . acknowledges the being of a God and believes in a future state of rewards and punishments."[43]
- The Constitution of Tennessee (1797): "No person who denies the being of God, or a future state of rewards and punishments, shall hold any office in the civil department of this State."[44]
- The U.S. Constitution requires a Christian oath, acknowledges the Christian Sabbath, and is dated in the year of our Lord.[45]
- The Northwest Ordinance (1789): Article III: "Religion, morality, and knowledge being necessary to good government and the happiness of mankind, schools and the means of education shall forever be encouraged."[46]

4. Christian nature of societal institutions of family, education, economics, private organizations

The history and nature of the societal institutions in the United States reflect Biblical values and the Christian environment in which they developed. This is true of the three divine institutions of family, church, and state, as well as other institutions that flow out of these three, such as education, business and economics, private associations, health and welfare. In recent years as we as a nation have moved toward socialism and humanism, the unbiblical ideas embodied in these worldviews have reshaped many institutions, and continue to pressure them to change (evidenced recently in the attempt to redefine marriage). However, for most of our history they have been thoroughly Christian.

The nature, purpose, order, authority, and goals of American families have primarily been Christian throughout our history.[47] Education in America has reflected a Christian philosophy. Schools were started to teach people to read the Bible; al-

In early America, the people made the laws and the churches made the people.

most all early colleges were started by a particular Christian denomination or for a religious reason; the most influential textbooks in the first three plus centuries of our history were thoroughly Christian.[48] (See Appendix 1.) From our early years, America embraced and developed a Christian view of economics.[49]

The New England Primer taught the alphabet with rhyming Biblical text.

America has led the way historically in the development of private volunteer organizations that have met the social needs of the nation, from assisting the poor, to distributing Bibles, educating the less fortunate, providing medical

Education in early America was Biblical in content, philosophy, and form.

needs, and scores of other things. In the 1830s, Alexis DeTocqueville observed there were multitudes of private organizations started by Americans all over the country to meet the needs of the citizens. What was attempted to be done by governments in Europe, he observed, was done by the private sector in America, and with much better results.[50]

5. Christian thought and life of the Founders

The Founders of America, the leaders and regular citizens, had a Biblical worldview and a living Christian faith. Almost everyone in early America was a Christian (we cannot know the heart of all early Americans — hence, some who culturally embraced Christianity may not have been genuine converted believers — but we can know their words and actions).[51] In 1838 the Legislature of New York said:

> Our Government depends for its being on the virtue of the people, – on that virtue that has its foundation in the morality of the Christian religion; and that religion is the common and prevailing faith of the people.[52]

The U.S. Senate adopted a report in 1853 that stated: "We are a Christian people — from the fact that almost our entire population belong to or sympathize with some one of the Christian denominations which compose the Christian world."[53]

A flag of the American Revolution.

America's Founders and Their Gospel Testimony

Most of the leaders in early America were Christians. They were from many denominations, some more outspoken in their faith than others, but almost all embraced the Christian faith. This included the more famous, as George Washington, Patrick Henry, Samuel Adams, James Madison, Benjamin Rush, John Witherspoon, and George Mason, but also those not well known today, such as Thomas McKean, James McHenry, and Zephaniah Swift. In fact, all but two or three of the men who signed the Declaration and Constitution were orthodox believers, and those who were not Christian generally had a Biblical worldview (for example, Benjamin Franklin).

America's Founders not only had a Biblical worldview, but they also had a living Biblical faith that they wanted to share with others. They presented the Gospel to others with the desire of converting them to Christ. This was not just done by ministers at church or at religious meetings, but in many different ways.

(1) Execution Sermons

Sermons were often preached at executions of criminals, calling them and the audience to salvation. Two examples are:

- *A Sermon Delivered at Salem, January 14, 1796, Occasioned by the Execution of Henry Blackburn, on that Day, for the Murder of George Wilkinson.* By Nathaniel Fisher, Rector of Saint Peter's Church, Salem. Published at the Desire of

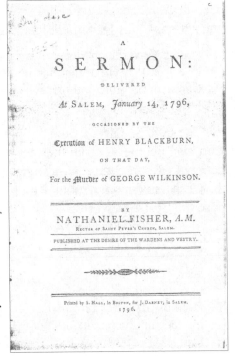

A

SERMON:

DELIVERED

At SALEM, *January* 14, 1796,

OCCASIONED BY THE

Execution of HENRY BLACKBURN,

ON THAT DAY,

For the Murder of GEORGE WILKINSON.

BY

NATHANIEL FISHER, *A. M.*

RECTOR OF SAINT PETER'S CHURCH, SALEM.

PUBLISHED AT THE DESIRE OF THE WARDENS AND VESTRY.

Printed by S. HALL, in BOSTON, for J. DABNEY, in SALEM.
1796.

the Wardens and Vestry, Boston: S. Hall, 1796.

- *A Sermon Preached in Hartford, June 10th, 1797, at the Execution of Richard Doane.* By Nathan Strong, Minister of the North Presbyterian Church in Hartford. To Which is Added, a Short Account of His Life, as Given by Himself: Also of the State of His Mind During the Time of His Confinement, and at His Death. Hartford: Elisha Babcock, 1797.[54]

(2) Last Will and Testaments

The Founders' firm Christian faith and their eagerness to communicate this to their posterity is evident in their wills.

Patrick Henry stated in his will, after instructions for distributing his personal property: "This is all the inheritance I can give to my dear family. The religion of Christ can give them one which will make them rich indeed."[55]

Richard Stockton, Signer of Declaration, as he was dying from hardships of captivity during the war, put his affairs in order, writing in his last will and testament:

As my children will have frequent occasion of perusing this instrument, and may probably be particularly impressed with the last words of their father, I think it proper here not only to subscribe to the entire belief of the great and leading doctrines of the Christian religion, such as the being of God; the universal defection and depravity of human nature; the Divinity of the person and the completeness of the redemption purchased by the blessed Savior; the necessity of the operations of the

Divine Spirit; of Divine faith accompanied with an habitual virtuous life; and the universality of the Divine Providence; but also, in the bowels of a father's affection, to exhort and charge [my children] that the fear of God is the beginning of wisdom, that the way of life held up in the Christian system is calculated for the most complete happiness that can be enjoyed in this mortal state, [and] that all occasions of vice and immorality is injurious either immediately or consequentially—even in this life.[56]

Samuel Adams, Father of the American Revolution, Signer of Declaration, stated in his will: "I rely upon the merits of Jesus Christ for a pardon of all my sins."[57]

In his will, **John Jay**, Chief Justice of the U.S. Supreme Court, one of the authors of the Federalist, wrote:

> Unto Him who is the Author and Giver of all good, I render sincere and humble thanks for His manifold and unmerited blessings and especially for our redemption and salvation by His beloved Son. . . . Blessed be His holy name![58]

George Mason, the Father of the Bill of Rights, stated in his last will and testament:

> My soul I resign into the hands of my Almighty Creator. Whose tender mercies are all over His works, . . . humbly hoping from His unbounded mercy and benevolence thro' the merits of my blessed Savior a remission of my sins.[59]

Robert Treat Paine, Signer of Declaration, plainly expressed his faith in his will:

> I am constrained to express my adoration of the Supreme Being, the Author of my existence, in full belief of His providential goodness and His forgiving mercy revealed to the world through Jesus Christ, through Whom I hope for never-ending happiness in a future state.[60]

John Dickinson, Revolutionary general and Signer of Constitution, wrote: "Rendering thanks to my Creator . . . to Him I resign myself, humbly confiding in His goodness and in His mercy through Jesus Christ for the events of eternity."[61]

(3) Writings

The Founders expressed their Christian faith in letters, speeches, and various writings. A few examples follow.

Charles Carroll, Signer of the Declaration: "On the mercy of my Redeemer I rely for salvation, and on His merits; not on the works that I have done in obedience to His precepts."[62]

Roger Sherman, Signer of the Declaration and Constitution:

> I believe that there is one only living and true God, existing in three persons, the Father, the Son, and the Holy Ghost. . . . that the Scriptures of the Old and New Testaments are a revelation from God. . . . that God did send His own Son to become man, die in the room and stead of sinners, and thus to lay a foundation for the offer of pardon and salvation to all mankind so as all may be saved who are willing to accept the Gospel offer.[63]

Benjamin Rush, Signer of the Declaration:

> My only hope of salvation is in the infinite, transcendent love of God manifested to the world by the death of His Son upon the cross. Nothing but His blood will wash away my sins. I rely exclusively upon it. Come, Lord Jesus! Come quickly![64]

(4) Graduation Speeches

William Samuel Johnson was a signer of the U.S. Constitution and the first President of

Columbia (King's) College. His words at a graduation ceremony reflect His faith.

> You this day . . . have, by the favor of Providence and the attention of friends, received a public education, the purpose whereof hath been to qualify you the better to serve your Creator and your country. You have this day invited this audience to witness the progress you have made. . . . Thus you assume the character of scholars, of men, and of citizens. . . . Go, then, . . . and exercise them with diligence, fidelity, and zeal. . . . Your first great duties, you are sensible, are those you owe to Heaven, to your Creator and Redeemer. Let these be ever present to your minds, and exemplified in your lives and conduct. Imprint deep upon your minds the principles of piety towards God, and a reverence and fear of His holy name. The fear of God is the beginning of wisdom and its [practice] is everlasting [happiness]. . . . Reflect deeply and often upon [your] relations [with God]. Remember that it is in God you live and move and have your being,—that, in the language of David, He is about your bed and about your path and spieth out all your ways,—that there is not a thought in your hearts, nor a word upon your tongues, but lo! He knoweth them altogether, and that He will one day call you to a strict account for all your conduct in this mortal life. Remember, too, that you are the redeemed of the Lord, that you are bought with a price, even the inestimable price of the precious blood of the Son of God. Adore Jehovah, therefore, as your God and your Judge. Love, fear, and serve Him as your Creator, Redeemer, and Sanctifier. Acquaint yourselves with Him in His word and holy ordinances. . . . [G]o forth into the world firmly resolved neither to be allured by its vanities nor contaminated by its vices, but to run with patience and perseverance, with firmness and [cheerfulness], the glorious career of religion, honor, and virtue. . . . Finally,. . . in the elegant and expressive language of St. Paul, 'Whatsoever things are true, whatsoever things are honest, whatsoever things are just, whatsoever things are pure, whatsoever things are lovely, whatsoever things are of good report, if there be any virtue, and if there be any praise, think on these things' — and do them,

and the God of peace shall be with you, to whose most gracious protection I now commend you, humbly imploring Almighty Goodness that He will be your guardian and your guide, your protector and the rock of your defence, your Savior and your God.[65]

Imagine the response this would receive today if such an address was given at the graduation at a major university. And that would be nothing compared to the response the following incident would bring.

(5) Courts

Thomas McKean — a signer of the Declaration, helped author the constitutions of Pennsylvania and Delaware, governor of each of these states, legal authority (writing *Commentaries on the Constitution of the United States of America*, 1792), Chief Justice of the Supreme Court of Pennsylvania — presided as Chief Justice over a trial where John Roberts was sentenced to death for treason. After delivering the sentence Chief Justice McKean gave this advice to Roberts:

> You will probably have but a short time to live. Before you launch into eternity, it behooves you to improve the time that may be allowed you in this world: it behooves you most seriously to reflect upon your past conduct; to repent of your evil deeds; to be incessant in prayers to the great and merciful God to forgive your manifold transgressions and sins; to teach you to rely upon the merit and passion of a dear Redeemer, and thereby to avoid those regions of sorrow—those doleful shades where peace and rest can never dwell, where even hope cannot enter. It behooves you to seek the [fellowship], ad-

All but 2 or 3 of the men who signed the Declaration were Christians.

vice, and prayers of pious and good men; to be [persistent] at the Throne of Grace, and to learn the way that leadeth to happiness. May you, reflecting upon these things, and pursuing the will of the great Father of light and life, be received into [the] company and society of angels and archangels and the spirits of just men made perfect; and may you be qualified to enter into the joys of Heaven—joys unspeakable and full of glory![66]

(6) Personal conversion testimonies

Noah Webster was the Founding Father of American Education, authoring numerous texts (the "Blue-Back" Speller, grammar, reader, history, and others), was a contributor to U.S. Constitution (securing copyright laws, presenting ideas to Washington and others on the general framework of new government, writing a paper in support of the document), was the author of the first exhaustive dictionary (first published in 1828), and was the founder of a college, a magazine, and a newspaper.

Noah Webster

For the first fifty years of Webster's life, he was a God-fearing, moral man who studied the Scriptures, attended church, and looked at life primarily from a Biblical perspective. Yet, it was not until 1808, shortly after his beginning work on the dictionary, that Webster repented and accepted salvation by faith.

That year, as revival swept through New Haven, his wife and two eldest daughters were three of the first to have their lives transformed. At first, Webster tried to rationalize what happened to his family as mere over-enthusiasm, but as the weeks went by his mind was more and more filled with thoughts of God, making his studies very difficult.

Webster described what happened one day while at his studies in a letter to his brother-in-law, Judge Thomas Dawes:

My mind was suddenly arrested, without any previous circumstance of the time to draw it to this subject and, as it were, fastened to the awakening and upon my own conduct. I closed my books, yielded to the influence which could not be resisted or mistaken, and was led by a spontaneous impulse to repentance, prayer, and entire submission and surrender of myself to my Maker and Redeemer. My submission appeared to be cheerful, and was soon followed by that peace of mind which the world can neither give nor take away.[67]

His already developed diligence is revealed by his action immediately following this, for "he instantly made known to his family the feelings which he entertained. He called them together the next morning and told them, with deep emotion, that, while he had aimed at the faithful discharge of all his duties as their parent and head, he had neglected one of the most important, that of family prayer. After reading the Scriptures, he led them, with deep solemnity, to the throne of grace, and from that time continued the practice, with the liveliest interest, to the period of his death."[68]

In editions of Webster's dictionary that were published after his death, an introductory biography of his life by his son-in-law was printed, so that everyone could learn of this great and influential man. This contained his conversion experience (see Appendix 2).[69]

6. The Christian power and form of our government

Both the power and form of the government of the United States are Biblical. The power is the internal principles and ideas embodied in our laws and constitutions. The form is the external framework of our Constitution. Our Founders understood the Christian nature of our government and wrote much about it.[70]

7. Testimony of public actions and words

Examining various public words and actions in our history add to the evidence that America was founded as a Christian nation. These include various court rulings, state papers, public proclamations, congressional action, newspapers, holidays, use of oaths, and public funding of chaplains.

Court Rulings

- *Church of the Holy Trinity v. United States* (1892): In its ruling, the U.S. Supreme Court declared "this is a Christian nation" and presented much historical evidence for this.[71]

- *Updegraph v. The Commonwealth* (1824): The Supreme Court of Pennsylvania ruled, "Christianity, general Christianity, is and always has been a part of the common law. . .; not Christianity with an established church . . . but Christianity with liberty of conscience to all men."[72]

- *The People v. Ruggles* (1811): In this decision delivered by Chief Justice James Kent, the Supreme Court of New York said "we are a Christian people and the morality of the country is deeply engrafted upon Christianity

The Supreme Court ruled that "this is a Christian nation" in 1892.

and not upon the doctrines or worship of those impostors [other religions]."[73]

- *Vidal v. Girard's Executors* (1844): "It is also said, and truly, that the Christian religion is a part of the common law."[74]

- *Runkel v. Winemiller* (1799): the Supreme Court of Maryland ruled, "By our form of government, the Christian religion is the established religion."[75]

- *City of Charleston v. Benjamin* (1846): "Christianity is a part of the common law of the land." "What constitutes the standard of good morals? Is it not Christianity? There certainly is none other. . . . The day of moral virtue in which we live would, in an instant, if that standard were abolished, lapse into the dark and murky night of Pagan immorality."[76]

- *Lindenmuller v. The People* (1860): The Supreme Court of New York ruled, "All agreed that the Christian religion was engrafted upon the law and entitled to protection as the basis of our morals and the strength of our government."[77]
- *Shover v. State* (1850): the Supreme Court of Arkansas ruled "the Christian religion . . . is recognized as constituting a part and parcel of the common law."[78]

Days of Public Prayer

Official government proclamations for days of prayer and thanksgiving and prayer and fasting have been a regular part of American history. As most early Americans embraced the doctrine of Divine Providence, they believed God's blessings would come upon those who obey His commands and curses would come upon the disobedient (see Deuteronomy 28 and Leviticus 26). This is why during times of calamity or crisis both church and civil authorities would proclaim days of fasting and prayer; and when God responded with deliverance and blessing, they would proclaim days of

Broadside ordering the fast day of September 22, 1670. This is possibly the first printed broadside in Massachusetts, and all the colonies, for a day of prayer. The numerous proclamations before this were written by hand.

thanksgiving and prayer. Such days of appeal to God were not rare, but a regular part of life in early America.

In *The Fast and Thanksgiving Days of New England*, W. DeLoss Love, Jr. lists thousands of these days that were proclaimed by governments and churches in New England from 1620 until 1815. Love records the history of how these days originated and gives many specific examples of events, historical and natural, that precipitated official proclamations.[79] The number of proclamations for public days of fasting or thanksgiving by governments at all levels (local, state, and national, with most issued on the state level) include: over 1000 from 1620–1776; about 60 from 1776–1788; and over 225 from 1789–1815. Such proclamations have continued up until today. (See Appendix 6 for two early examples.)

During observance of fast and thanksgiving days, people would gather at their local meeting houses and churches to hear a sermon. Many of these sermons were printed and distributed for study. Love's bibliography includes 622 fast and thanksgiving day sermons that were published, dating from 1636 to 1815.

Rev. Jacob Duché opened the The First Continental Congress in prayer, September 1774.

Action of the First Congresses

The early national congresses undertook many actions that reflect their Christian character. A few of them include:

- They issued proclamations for 13 days of prayer and fasting or thanksgiving during the American Revolution.
- They authorized chaplains to open their sessions in prayer; starting with the first Continental Congress in September 1774.
- They appointed chaplains for Congress and authorized the army to do so as well (see Appendix 7).
- They authorized the importation of 20,000 Bibles during the Revolution, since, they said, "the use of the Bible is so universal and its importance so great."

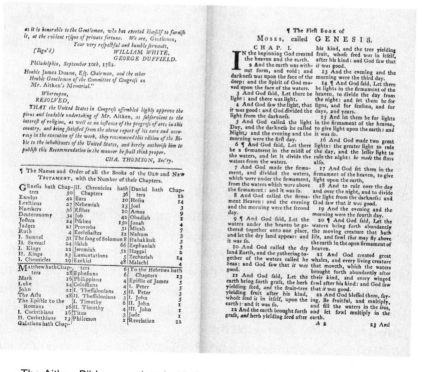

The Aitken Bible was printed with Congressional approval: "Whereupon, Resolved, That the United States in Congress assembled . . . recommend this edition of the Bible to the inhabitants of the United States."

- They officially approved the printing and distribution of "the Bible of the Revolution," an American translation prepared by Robert Aitken (known as the Aitken Bible).
- At special events they would attend church services as a body.
- They approved the use of the Capitol Building for church services, with many of them regularly attending.[80]

Celebrating Independence Day in 1876. John Adams said such days should be celebrated "by solemn acts of devotion to God Almighty."

American Holidays are Holy Days

Most of America's holidays reflect our Christian faith. Our holidays used to be referred to as holydays, because God was always remembered on these days. This is obvious for Christmas and Easter, but knowing the true history of the men and events we honor and remember on other holidays also reveals our Christian foundations. The unique American holiday of Thanksgiving is rooted in the Pilgrims expressing their gratefulness to God. John Adams said he believed the day of Independence "will be celebrated, by succeeding generations . . . as the day of deliverance, by solemn acts of devotion to God Almighty, . . . from one end of this continent to the other, from this time forward forever more."[81] On Washington's and Lincoln's birthdays (they used to be celebrated as separate holidays), and on Columbus Day we celebrate the lives of Christian men whom God used for His providential purposes. On Memorial Day we honor those who have paid the price for liberty — liberty which is a product of Christianity.

Public Sermons

Various types of public sermons have been a part of American life since our beginning. Execution Sermons and Fast and Thanksgiving Day sermons were mentioned above. Election Sermons, which were preached before newly elected officials, began in Massachusetts in 1633 and

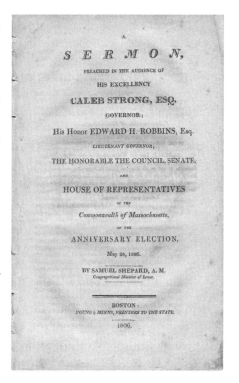

An election sermon preached in Massachusetts, May 28, 1806.

lasted for over 250 years. These were often printed, widely distributed, and served as their "political textbooks." In addition, there were also many sermons preached on special anniversaries and events. (See Appendix 5.)

Observance of the Sabbath

The Christian Sabbath has been observed and recognized by law from the beginning of America. Sabbath laws could be found in all the early colonies and states. Alexis de Tocqueville described the Sabbath observance of the 1830s in *Democracy in America:*

> In the United States, on the seventh day of every week, the trading and working life of the nation seems suspended; all noises cease; a deep tranquillity, say rather the solemn calm of meditation, succeeds the turmoil of the week, and the soul resumes possession and

contemplation of itself. Upon this day the marts of traffic are deserted; every member of the community, accompanied by his children, goes to church, where he listens to strange language which would seem unsuited to his ear. He is told of the countless evils caused by pride and covetousness: he is reminded of the necessity of checking his desires, of the finer pleasures which belong to virtue alone, and of the true happiness which attends it. On his return home, he does not turn to the ledgers of his calling, but he opens the book of Holy Scripture; there he meets with sublime or affecting descriptions of the greatness and goodness of the Creator, of the infinite magnificence of the handiwork of God, of the lofty destinies of man, of his duties, and of his immortal privileges. Thus it is that the American at times steals an hour from himself; and laying aside for a while the petty passions which agitate his life, and the ephemeral interests which engross it, he strays at once into an ideal world, where all is great, eternal, and pure.[82]

In 1853, a Senate Judiciary Committee examined the role of Christianity in the history of our nation and adopted a report strongly affirming America's traditional, non-denominational reliance on Christianity, in which they said "that Sunday, the Christian Sabbath, is recognized and respected by all the departments of the Government." They went on to explain that

in the law, Sunday is a "dies non;" it cannot be used for the service of legal process, the return of writs, or other judicial purposes. The executive departments, the public establishments, are all closed on Sundays; on that day neither House of Congress sits. . . . Here is a recognition by law, and by universal usage, not only of a Sabbath but of the Christian Sabbath, in exclusion of the Jewish or Mohammedan Sabbath. . . . The recognition of the Christian Sabbath is complete and perfect.[83]

The Biblical quote, "Proclaim Liberty throughout all the land, unto all the inhabitants thereof. Lev. XXV X" is engraved on the Liberty Bell.

8. The fruit of obedience to the precepts of Christianity produced liberty, prosperity, and service.

If we had no knowledge of the evidence presented above, but understood the nature of the fruit produced by obedience to God, we would have to conclude that those who birthed America sought to obey His will, for no nation has exhibited as much liberty and prosperity as the United States. America's Founders believed what the Bible teaches, that obedience to the law of God produces freedom, prosperity, and advancement, as well as a desire to spread liberty and aid others. They understood Christianity produced liberty of all kinds — personal, civil, religious, political, and economic. They also believed that religion affects the form of government in a nation. In a general sense they saw Christianity as the only support for a free, self-governed, and happy society. Consider the following statements.

John Adams said while President in 1798:

> [W]e have no government armed with power capable of contending with human passions unbridled by morality and religion. Avarice, ambition, revenge, or gallantry, would break the strongest cords of our Constitution as a whale goes through a net. Our Constitution was made only for a moral and religious people. It is wholly inadequate to the government of any other.[84]

In 1838 the Legislature of New York said:

> Our Government depends for its being on the virtue of the people, – on that virtue that has its foundation in the morality of the Christian religion; and that religion is the common and prevailing faith of the people.[85]

George Washington wrote in 1797: "Religion and Morality are the essential pillars of Civil society."[86] In his farewell address in 1796, he wrote: "Of all the dispositions and habits which lead to political prosperity, religion and morality are indispensable supports."[87]

George Washington

James Madison wrote in 1825: "[T]he belief in a God All Powerful wise and good, is...essential to the moral order of the World and to the happiness of man."[88] In his *Memorial and Remonstrance*, he said, "Before any man can be considered as a member of Civil Society, he must be considered as a subject of the Governor of the Universe."[89]

James Madison

Noah Webster wrote in his *History of the United States*, "the genuine source of correct republican principles is the Bible, particularly the New Testament or the Christian religion."[90]

Benjamin Rush wrote in 1806: "Christianity is the only true and perfect religion, and that in proportion as mankind adopt its principles and obey its precepts, they will be wise and happy."[91]

The Father of American Geography, **Jedidiah Morse** wrote: "To the kindly influence of Christianity we owe that degree of civil freedom, and political and social happiness which mankind now enjoys."[92]

The Constitution of New Hampshire of June 2, 1784 stated:

> [M]orality and piety, rightly grounded on evangelical principles, will give the best and greatest security to government, and will lay in the hearts of men the strongest obligations to due subjection.[93]

James McHenry, signer of the Constitution said:

> The Holy Scriptures . . . can alone secure to society, order and peace, and to our courts of justice and constitutions of government, purity, stability, and usefulness. In vain, without the Bible, we increase penal laws and draw entrenchments around our institutions.[94]

Samuel Adams stated: "Religion and good morals are the only solid foundations of public liberty and happiness."[95]

Charles Carroll, Signer of the Declaration, wrote:

> Without morals a republic cannot subsist any length of time; they therefore who are decrying the Christian religion whose morality is so sublime and pure . . . are undermining the solid foundation of morals, the best security for the duration of free governments.[96]

Thomas Jefferson wrote in 1809:

Thomas Jefferson

> The practice of morality being necessary for the well-being of society, He [God] has taken care to impress its precepts so indelibly on our hearts that they shall not be effaced by the subtleties of our brain. We all agree in the obligation of the moral precepts of Jesus and nowhere will they be found delivered in greater purity than in his discourses.[97]

Many other Founders could be quoted to show that the generally accepted view of early America was that the Christian religion was the foundation of liberty and our free republican form of government. Early courts and congresses declared the same thing. For example, the **U.S. House of Representatives** resolved in 1854, "the great vital and conservative element in our system is the belief of our people in the pure doctrines and divine truths of the gospel of Jesus Christ."[98]

Why did early Americans believe Christianity was essential to free government? They believed it contained the principles of liberty, and also the power to transform men from within to live as self-governed citizens. The Supreme Court of New York ruled (in People v. Ruggles, 1811), "whatever strikes at the root of Christianity tends manifestly to the dissolution of civil government . . . because it tends to corrupt the morals of the people, and to destroy good order."[99]

Thomas Jefferson noted:

The precepts of philosophy, and of the Hebrew code, laid hold of actions only. [Jesus] pushed his scrutinies into the heart of man, erected his tribunal in the region of his thoughts, and purified the waters at the fountain head.[100]

Montesquieu

To our Founders, the religion of a people affected their civil and religious liberty. To them, Christianity laid the support for free governments in general, but it also affected the specific form of government. In *The Spirit of Laws*, Montesquieu presented the idea that a nation's form of civil government is directly determined by its religion. Under the section on "Of Laws in Relation to Religion Considered in Itself, and in its Doctrines," he writes:

The Christian religion, which ordains that men should love each other, would, without doubt, have every nation blest with the best civil, the best political laws; because these, next to this religion, are the greatest good that men can give and receive.[101]

He goes on to make the points, under titled sections: 1) "That a moderate Government is most agreeable to the Christian Religion, and a despotic Government to the Mahommedan" and 2) "That the Catholic Religion is most agreeable to a Monarchy, and the

Matthew Maury   Samuel F.B. Morse   Cyrus McCormick

Protestant to a Republic"[102] These are important ideas that should be explored by nations seeking to be free.

Personal, religious, and civil liberty in America made economic liberty possible. Freedom to work and invent, and benefit from the fruit of that labor, encouraged many advances leading to economic prosperity. Christian men led the way in this, as seen by Cyrus McCormick and the invention of the reaper,[103] Samuel F.B. Morse and the telegraph,[104] Matthew Fontaine Maury and his wind and sea charts, and George Washington Carver and the progression of agriculture.[105]

George Washington Carver

9. The Central role of the Bible

On June 8, 1845, President Andrew Jackson said that "the Bible is the rock on which our Republic rests." Early Americans would almost universally agree that the religious, social, educational, and political life of America was primarily shaped by the Bible. Our states were colonized by people who desired to freely worship the God of the Bible; our schools were begun so that everyone would be able to read and understand the Bible for themselves; our universities

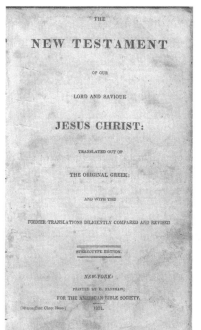

A Bible printed by the American Bible Society in 1831. 35 Bible Societies joined together in 1816 to form the American Bible Society. Elias Boudinot, President of the Continental Congress in 1782, became its first President. 85 other local societies joined with it the first year. Without the Bible there would be no America as we know it today.

were founded to train ministers who were knowledgeable of the Scriptures; our laws and constitutions were written based on Biblical ideas; and our Founding Fathers overwhelmingly had a Biblical worldview. The Bible was the single most important influence in the lives of colonial Americans. This is what we would expect in a Christian nation since the Bible is central to Protestant Christianity.[106] To propagate the truth of the Bible, the Founders started and served in scores of Bible Societies (see Appendix 3). The sixth President, John Quincy Adams, was so concerned with his son learning the Bible that he wrote a series of letters to him on the Bible and its teachings. These letters were printed shortly after Adams death and widely distributed throughout America (see Appendix 4).

Pluralistic America

After considering the motive and Christian influence in colonization, the foundation and source of our law, the nature and content of specific laws, the Christian nature of societal institutions, the Christian thought and life of our Founders, the Christian power and form of our government, the testimony of public actions and words, the fruit produced in the American republic, and the central role of the Bible, we see that the evidence is overwhelming — America was founded as a Christian nation.

Some who have a knowledge of this evidence concede that we were Christian at one time, but they say this does not matter today, for we no longer are Christian. We are pluralistic, comprised of people of many faiths. To them we must, therefore, act as if Christianity is just one of many religions, and it must be kept out of influencing public affairs, and people who are

Washington taking the oath of office with his hand on the Bible.

Christian should keep their faith private. It is true that Christianity has greatly diminished in its role in America, but are we, therefore, to act as if it is irrelevant to our public life? How do we answer those who claim we are now pluralistic?

First, our Constitution still presupposes a Biblical view of law and life — in the words of Adams only a Christian people can provide the power to support it. Any change to this must come in a constitutional manner, not through activist judges, spurred on by instruction of misguided law schools. As we debate what changes we wish to enact, Americans must understand that the source of our liberty, law, and prosperity was Christianity. If we remove the foundation, we will remove the source of what has made America great. People who are attempting to remove God from public life are "slitting their own throats" because they are removing that which produced the liberty they now have (which they are wrongly using to speak out and attack God). If God is completely removed, there will be no more liberty or justice for all. (Remember the communist nations of the Twentieth Century.)

Second, a large majority of Americans still believe in God, that He created life, that the Ten Commandments should be on the walls of public buildings, and that children should be able to voluntarily pray in schools. A secular minority has been ruling over the majority views of Americans.

Third, all nations are built upon some religion, where law has as its source that which society considers as supreme. A religiously neutral state is a myth. We must choose which faith (source of law, standard for conduct, etc.) we want to have our nation built upon. Let's have an open debate on this so everyone can clearly understand the fundamental question we are deciding — Who will be our God as a nation. As this is considered, the American people must understand, in the words of Noah Webster, that

> Almost all the civil liberty now enjoyed in the world owes its origin
> to the principles of the Christian religion. . . The religion which has
> introduced civil liberty, is the religion of Christ and his apostles,
> which enjoins humility, piety, and benevolence; which acknowl-
> edges in every person a brother, or a sister, and a citizen with equal

rights. This is genuine Christianity, and to this we owe our free constitutions of government.[107]

The Changing Foundation of American Society

While America was strongly Christian in the beginning, the influence of Christianity has diminished, especially in the last century, through unbelief, corruption of doctrine and neglect of institutions.[108] These things led to a change in educational philosophy (in the home, church, and school), which in turn produced a change in many Americans' view of law and life, from Christian to humanistic. This humanistic worldview, adhered to by not only non-Christians but most Christians as well, has affected all of life — the nature and scope of civil government, the amount and types of taxation, the extent and nature of liberty, the role of state schools, etc.

America became the most free and prosperous nation in history due to our Christian foundation. We are still the most free and prosperous nation in the world, but we have been living off of the capital or fruit of Christianity for some time. We cannot continue to do so, but must reestablish Christian principles as the foundation of the nation if we hope to remain free and prosperous.

The great Christian statesmen of the Nineteenth Century, Daniel Webster, gave us this warning:

Daniel Webster

If we and our posterity shall be true to the Christian religion, if we and they shall live always in the fear of God and shall respect His Commandments, . . . we may have the highest hopes of the future fortunes of our country; . . . . But if we and our posterity neglect religious instruction and authority, violate the rules of eternal justice, trifle with the injunctions of morality, and recklessly destroy the political constitution which holds us together, no man can tell how sudden a catastrophe may overwhelm us that shall bury all our glory in profound obscurity.[109]

The future of America is dependent upon us understanding our history and being eternally vigilant to uphold the ideals upon which our Founders established this great nation. ■

Worship of God and propagation of the Gospel were a central part of the foundation of America. Pictured below: the first church services at Jamestown were held outside under the trees (upper left); the baptism of Pocahontas (upper right); the Pilgrims worship at the church in Plymouth (below).

Appendix 1

Christian Content of Early American Textbooks

The Colonial Hornbook was used to teach reading throughout the 1600s. A hornbook was a flat piece of wood with a handle, upon which a sheet of printed paper was attached and covered with transparent animal horn to protect it. A typical hornbook had the alphabet, the vowels, a list of syllables, the invocation of the Trinity, and the Lord's Prayer. Some, like this one, had a pictured alphabet.

WHAT's right and good now shew me Lord, and lead me by thy grace and word. Thus shall I be a child of God, and love and fear thy hand and rod.

An Alphabet of Lessons for Youth.

A Wise son maketh a glad father, but a foolish son is the heaviness of his mother.

B Etter is a little with the fear of the Lord, than great treasure & trouble therewith.

C Ome unto Christ all ye that labor and are heavy laden and he will give you rest.

D O not the abominable thing which I hate faith the Lord.

E Xcept a man be born again, he cannot see the kingdom of God.

F Oolishness is bound up in the heart of a child, but the rod of correction shall drive it far from him.

G ODLINESS is profitable unto all things, having the promise of the life that now is, and that which is to come.

H OLINESS becomes G O D's house for ever.

I T is good for me to draw near unto G O D.

K EEP thy heart with all diligence, for out of it are the issues of life.

L IARS shall have their part in the lake which burns with fire and brimstone.

M ANY are the afflictions of the righteous, but the L O R D delivereth them out of them all.

N OW is the accepted time, now is the day of salvation.

O UT of the abundance of the heart the mouth speaketh.

P RAY to thy Father which is in secret; and thy Father which sees in secret shall reward thee openly.

Q UIT you like men, be strong, stand fast in the faith.

R EMEMBER thy Creator in the days of thy youth.

S Eeft thou a man wife in his own conceit, there is more hope of a fool than of him.

T RUST in God at all times, ye people, pour out your hearts before him.

U PON the wicked, God shall rain an horrible tempest.

W O to the wicked, it shall be ill with him, for the reward of his hands shall be given him.

The New England Primer was first published in Boston around 1690 by devout Protestant Benjamin Harris. It was the most promient schoolbook for about 100 years. It sold over 3 million copies in 150 years. Its content was thoroughly Christian, as seen by this alphabet lesson for youth.

SPELLING-BOOK. 101

MOVE, SON, WOLF, FOOT, MOON, OR; RULE, PULL; EXIST; C=K; G=J; S=Z; CH=SH.

cold there condenses these vapors into thick clouds, which fall in showers of rain.
Noah and his family outlived all the people who lived before the flood.
The brave sailors embark on board of ships, and sail over the great and deep sea.
The time will soon come when we must bid a last farewell to this world.
The bright stars without number adorn the skies.
When our friends die, they will never return to us; but we must soon follow them.
God will forgive those who repent of their sins, and live a holy life.
Thy testimonies, O Lord, are very sure; holiness becometh thine house for ever.
Do not attempt to deceive God; nor to mock him with solemn words, whilst your heart is set to do evil.
A holy life will disarm death of its sting.
God will impart grace to the humble penitent

Part of Lesson No. 109 in Webster's "Blue Back Speller" (1880 edition). Webster's speller, first published in 1783, sold over 100 million copies in a century. It was the most influential textbook of the era and reflected the Biblical worldview of its author.

DIVISIONS OF HISTORY.

A. The history of the creation, as recorded by Moses in the first chapter of Genesis; comprising the formation of all those vast and luminous worlds that fill the unbounded extent of heaven with their majesty and splendor, the sun, the earth, the moon and stars innumerable; the creation of animate nature, with man for its head, the covenant between man and his God; man's violation of that covenant which brought death into the world and all our woe; the early promise to man that the seed of the woman should bruise the serpent's head, and that man should be restored to the lost favour of his God.
Q. What do we know of God, and his character?
A. The character of God is best explained and understood by his works of nature and volume of Revelation. God is known to us by his attributes, and he may have many others beyond our comprehension. "Who by searching can find out God." Job. xi. 7, 8, 9.
Q. What general knowledge have we of the character of God?
A. That he conceived of all nature, material and immaterial, animate and inanimate, in heaven, earth, and worlds innumerable that fill the immensity of space, and by his almighty fiat spoke them into being.
Q. What particular knowledge have we of his character?
A. That he regulates and controls all the events of the universe by his superintending

USE OF HISTORY.

Providence; that the smallest, as well as the largest events are equally the objects of his care; not a sparrow falls to the ground without his notice, and, even the hairs of our heads are all numbered.
Q. What evidence have we of this?
A. The events predicted by the prophets, (through the inspiration of God,) and recorded in the sacred volume, hundreds and thousands of years before their accomplishment; and the exact and particular accomplishment of those events, as recorded by historians, from the earliest ages of the world down to this day, all confirm this truth; and further, that God regards all the particular parts of the universe as minutely as though there was but one; and the whole with that general order and harmony, as if it had no parts.
Q. What is the use of history?
A. To expand the mind of man, and lead it up to God; as the great author, preserver, and governor of all things.
Q. What are we to understand by sacred history?
A. That which relates to the church of God; beginning with the call of Abraham, and continuing to the time of the Messiah, or CHRIST; and from thence, to the end of the world.
Q. What are we to understand by profane history?
A. A narrative of the transactions of men, generally and individually; comprising the rise and fall of nations, kingdoms, and empires.

Frederick Butler's *General History* (1818) was the first general history for the use of schools published in America. Butler wrote that part of the purpose of the book was "to lead the youthful mind to a correct knowledge of the providence and government of God." The questions above relate an overview of history at the beginning of Chapter 1.

Appendix 2

The Conversion of Noah Webster

though with some misgiving and frequent fluctuations of feeling, to the winter of 1807–8. At that time, there was a season of general religious interest at New Haven, under the ministry of the Rev. Moses Stuart, now a professor in the Andover Theological Seminary. To this Dr. Webster's attention was first directed, by observing an unusual degree of tenderness and solemnity of feeling in all the adult members of his family. He was thus led to reconsider his former views, and inquire, with an earnestness which he had never felt before, into the nature of personal religion, and the true ground of man's acceptance with God. He had now to decide not for himself only, but, to a certain extent, for others, whose spiritual interests were committed to his charge. Under a sense of this responsibility, he took up the study of the Bible with painful solicitude. As he advanced, the objections which he had formerly entertained against the humbling doctrines of the gospel, were wholly removed. He felt their truth in his own experience. He felt that salvation *must* be wholly of grace. He felt constrained, as he afterward told a friend, to cast himself down before God, confess his sins, implore pardon through the merits of the Redeemer, and there to make his vows of entire obedience to the commands and devotion to the service of his Maker. With his characteristic promptitude, he instantly made known to his family the feelings which he entertained. He called them together the next morning, and told them, with deep emotion, that, while he had aimed at the faithful discharge of all his duties as their parent and head, he had neglected one of the most important, that of family prayer. After reading the Scriptures, he led them, with deep solemnity, to the throne of grace, and from that time continued the practice, with the liveliest interest, to the period of his death. He made a public profession of religion in April, 1808. His two oldest daughters united with him in the act, and another, only twelve years of age, was soon added to the number.

The recording of the conversion of Noah Webster in an introductory article by Chauncey Goodrich in the 1860 edition of Webster's *An American Dictionary of the English Language*.

Appendix 3

America's Founders started and served as officers in numerous Bible societies. A few include:

- John Marshall, Vice-president of American Bible Society
- James McHenry (Signer of Constitution), President of the Baltimore Bible Society
- John Langdon (Signer of Constitution), VP of the American Bible Society
- Rufus King (Signer of Constitution). Member of N.Y. Bible Society
- John Quincy Adams, VP of the American Bible Society
- Elias Boudinot (President of the Continental Congress), Founder and first President of the American Bible Society, President of the N.J. Bible Society
- James Burrill, Jr. (Chief Justice of Rhode Island Supreme Court; U.S. Senator), President of the Providence Auxiliary Bible Society
- Dewitt Clinton (Governor NY; U.S. Senator), Manager and VP of the American Bible Society
- Caleb Strong (Constitutional Convention), VP of the American Bible Society
- John Hamilton (Major-General in the Revolution, U.S. Congress), Member of the N.J. Bible Society
- John Jay (Original Chief Justice of the U.S. Supreme Court), President of the American Bible Society
- Charles Cotesworth Pinckney (Signer of Constitution), President of the Charleston Bible Society, VP of American Bible Society
- Rufus Putnam (Rev. General, Federal Judge), President of the Ohio Bible Society
- Benjamin Rush (Signer of Declaration), Founder and manager of the Philadelphia Bible Society
- John Cotton Smith (Governor of Conn.; U.S. Congressman), First President of the Connecticut Bible Society
- Daniel Tompkins (Governor N.Y., VP of the United States), VP of the American Bible Society
- Bushrod Washington (U.S. Supreme Court Justice), VP of the American Bible Society

Appendix 4

Letters of John Quincy Adams on the Bible

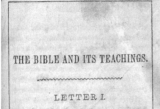

THE BIBLE AND ITS TEACHINGS.

LETTER I.

St. Petersburg, *Sept.*, 1811.

My Dear Son : In your letter of the 18th January to your mother, you mentioned that you read to your aunt a chapter in the Bible or a section of Doddridge's Annotations every evening. This information gave me real pleasure; for so great is my veneration for the Bible, and so strong my belief, that when duly read and meditated on, it is of all books in the world, that which contributes most to make men good, wise, and happy—that the earlier my children begin to read it, the more steadily they pursue the prac-

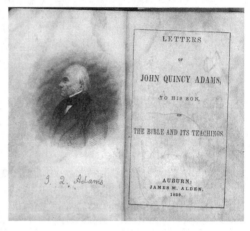

LETTERS

of

JOHN QUINCY ADAMS,

TO HIS SON,

on

THE BIBLE AND ITS TEACHINGS.

AUBURN:
JAMES M. ALDEN,
1850.

J. Q. Adams

While ambassador at St. Petersburg, Adams wrote a number of letters to one of his sons at school in Massachusetts. Their purpose was to inculcate a love and reverence for the Holy Scriptures. Here are the first 3 pages of the 1850 edition of the printing of the letters.

10   THE BIBLE

tice of reading it throughout their lives, the more lively and confident will be my hopes that they will prove useful citizens to their country, respectable members of society, and a real blessing to their parents. But I hope you have now arrived at an age to understand that reading, even in the Bible, is a thing in itself, neither good nor bad, but that all the good which can be drawn from it, is by the use and improvement of what you have read, with the help of your own reflection. Young people sometimes boast of how many books, and how much they have read; when, instead of boasting, they ought to be ashamed of having wasted so much time, to so little profit. I advise you, my son, in whatever you read, and most of all in reading the Bible, to remember that it is for the purpose of making you wiser and more virtuous. I have myself, for many years,

AND ITS TEACHINGS.   11

made it a practice to read through the Bible once every year. I have always endeavored to read it with the same spirit and temper of mind, which I now recommend to you : that is, with the intention and desire that it may contribute to my advancement in wisdom and virtue. My desire is indeed very imperfectly successful; for, like you, and like the Apostle Paul, " I find a law in my members, warring against the laws of my mind." But as I know that it is my nature to be imperfect, so I know that it is my duty to aim at perfection ; and feeling and deploring my own frailties, I can only pray Almighty God, for the aid of his Spirit to strengthen my good desires, and to subdue my propensities to evil; for it is from him, that every good and every perfect gift descends. My custom is, to read four or five chapters every morning, immediately after rising from my bed. It employs

Appendix 5

Sermons in Early America

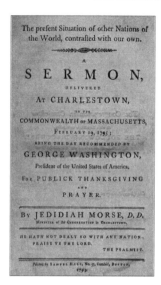

Christian ministers discipled early Americans in every sphere of life. They not only addressed personal and civil matters in regular Sunday sermons and in special Thanksgiving Day Sermons (above left), Artillery Sermons (above right), Election Sermons, Fast Day Sermons, and Execution Sermons, but they also addressed an all-encompassing view of life as seen in the sermons below — A discourse occasioned by an earthquake, "Moral View of Rail Roads," "A Sermon Containing Reflections on the Solar Eclipse." [sermons courtesy of WallBuilders]

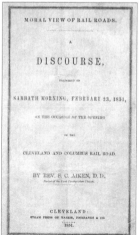

Appendix 6

Proclamation for a Day of Prayer and Thanksgiving

At A

COUNCIL,

Held at Charlestown, June the 20th, 1676.

The holy God having by a long and Continued Series of his Afflictive dispensations in & by the present Warr with the Heathen Natives of this Land, written and brought to pass bitter things against his own Covenant people in this wilderness, yet so that we evidently discern that in the midst of his judgements he hath remembred mercy, having remembred his Foot-Stool in the day of his sore displeasure against us for our sins, with many singular Intimations of his Fatherly Compassion, and regard: reserving many of our Towns from Desolation Threatned, and attempted by the Enemy, and giving us especially of late with our Confederates many signal Advantages against them, without such Disadvantage to our selves as formerly we have been sensible of, if it be of the Lords mercies that we are not consumed, It certainly bespeaks our positive Thankfulness, when our Enemies are in any measure disappointed or destroyed: and fearing the Lord should take notice under so many Intimations of his returning mercy, we should be found an Insensible people, as not standing before him with Thanksgiving, as well as lading him with our Complaints in the time of pressing Afflictions:

The COUNCIL have thought meet to appoint and set apart the 29th. day of this Instant June, as a day of Solemn Thanksgiving and praise to God for such his goodness and Favour, many Particulars of which mercy might be Instanced, but we doubt not those who are sensible of Gods Afflictions, have been as diligent to espy him returning to us; and that the Lord may behold us as a People offering praise and thereby glorifying him; The Council doth Commend it to the Respective Ministers, Elders and people of this Jurisdiction; Solemnly and seriously to keep the same. Beseeching that being perswaded by the mercies of God we may all, even this whole people offer up our Bodies and Souls as a living and Acceptable Service unto God by Jesus Christ.

By the Council, Edward Rawson Secr.

On June 20, 1676, the Council of Massachusetts appointed June 29 as a Day of Thanksgiving and Prayer, in response to the colonists' victory in King Philip's War. The printed broadside of this proclamation is the earliest thanksgiving broadside known. At the top is the seal of Massachusetts, which shows an Indian speaking the words, "Come Over and Help Us." [From W. DeLoss Love, Jr., *The Fast and Thanksgiving Days of New England*, New York: Houghton, Mifflin and Co., 1895.]

Massachusetts Day of Prayer, July 3, 1776

Resolve desiring the Council to appoint a Day of solemn Humiliation and Prayer; passed JULY 3, 1776.

It having been the laudable practice of this Government to recommend and appoint days for Fasting and Prayer upon solemn and special occasions; and as this Court apprehend that the present time is big with the most important events to this and the other Colonies, and that these events are at the disposal of the Supreme Governour of the Universe:

Therefore, *Resolved,* That the honourable Council be, and hereby are, desired to set apart *Thursday,* the last day of *July* instant, to be observed as a day of solemn Humiliation and Prayer, devoutly to implore of *Almighty God,* that the monitory dispensation of Providence, in the drought wherewith some parts of the land has been visited, and the humbling events which have lately taken place in *Canada,* may, accompanied with a Divine influence, produce a sincere repentance and thorough reformation of manners among all orders and degrees of persons; that He will command his blessing on our councils and arms at this important crisis of our publick affairs, and that this People, placing their hope and confidence in that *God* in whom their fathers trusted and were not made ashamed, may be moved and encouraged manfully and freely to offer themselves for the defence of those rights, civil and religious, upon the enjoyment of which the peace and happiness of the present and future generations absolutely depend; that He will, at a time of increased demand of provisions for the support of our brethren in the field, and when the usual foreign supplies are not to be obtained, be graciously pleased so to order the seasons as that we may have, in the course of this year, a sufficiency of the fruits of the earth, both for man and beast. And that they cause a Proclamation to be immediately issued and sent to the Ministers and Pastors of the several denominations of Christians in this Colony, for the purposes aforesaid.

During the Revolutionary War the national Congress declared at least 13 Days of Prayer & Fasting and Prayer & Thanksgiving. During this important period the various states proclaimed numerous Days of Prayer as well. Here is a Resolve for one such day that the Massachusetts Assemby passed on July 3, 1776, as found in *American Archives*, Peter Force, ed., Fifth Series, Vol. 1. 1848, 310.

Appendix 7

Chaplains in the Congress and Army

Correspondence, Proceedings, etc., of Congress, July, 1776, by John Hancock, President.

PRESIDENT OF CONGRESS TO REV. JACOB DUCHE.

Philadelphia, July 8, 1776.

SIR: It is with the greatest pleasure I inform you that the Congress have been induced, from a consideration of your

piety, as well as your uniform and zealous attachment to the rights of *America*, to appoint you their Chaplain.

It is their request, which I am commanded to signify to you, that you will attend on them every morning at nine o'clock.

I have the honour to be, sir, with respect, your most obedient and very humble servant,

JOHN HANCOCK, *President.*

To the Rev. Mr. *Jacob Duché.*

Chaplains have been a part of America's government and military from the beginning of the nation. Here are two official writings, one by Hancock appointing a chaplain for Congress, and the other by Washington giving directions for officers to procure chaplains for each regiment of the Continental Army. [From *American Archives*, Peter Force, ed., Fifth Series, Vol. 1. 1848, 116, 226.

General Orders of George Washington, Head-Quarters, New York, July 9, 1776.

The honourable Continental Congress having been pleased to allow a Chaplain to each Regiment, with the pay of thirty-three dollars and one-third per month, the Colonels or Commanding Officers of each Regiment are directed to procure Chaplains accordingly; persons of good character and exemplary lives; to see that all inferior officers and soldiers pay them a suitable respect, and attend carefully upon religious exercises. The blessing and protection of Heaven are at all times necessary, but especially so in times of publick distress and danger. The General hopes and trusts that every officer and man will endeavour so to live and act as becomes a Christian soldier defending the dearest rights and liberties of his country.

End Notes

1. B.F. Morris, *Christian Life and Character of the Civil Institutions of the United States*, Philadelphia: George W. Childs, 1864, pp. 318-328. The Senate Committee gave three aspects of a "law respecting an establishment of religion": 1. "Endowment [of a particular denomination or religion] at the public expense" 2. "Peculiar privileges to its members" 3. "Disadvantages or penalties upon those who should reject its doctrines or belong to other communions."

2. William Jay, *The Life of John Jay*, New York: J. & J. Harper, 1833, Vol. II, p. 376, to John Murray, Jr. on October 12, 1816.

3. Daniel L. Dreisbach, *Religion and Politics in the Early Republic*, Lexington, Ken.: The University Press of Kentucky, 1996, p. 113.

4. Morris, p. 239.

5. *Church of the Holy Trinity v. U.S.*; 143 U.S. 457, 458 (1892).

6. *Sources of Our Liberties*, Richard L. Perry, editor, New York: American Bar Foundation, 1952, p. 40.

7. *Sources of Our Liberties*, p. 60.

8. *Sources of Our Liberties*, p. 120.

9. The Charter of Maryland, June 20, 1632, in *Sources of Our Liberties*, p. 105.

10. *Sources of Our Liberties*, p. 169

11. *Colonial Origins of the American Constitution*, edited by Donald S. Lutz, Indianapolis: Liberty Fund, 1998, p. 35.

12. *Sources of Our Liberties*, p. 209.

13. *Sources of Our Liberties*, p. 256.

14. *Colonial Origins of the American Constitution*, pp. xxxv-xxxvi.

15. Donald S. Lutz, "The Relative Influence of European Writers on Late Eighteenth-Century American Political Thought," *The American Political Science Review*, vol. 78, 1984, pp. 189-197. See Stephen McDowell, *Building Godly Nations*, Charlottesville: Providence Foundation, 2004, pp. 185-190, for quotes from these political writers that show their Christian view of law.

16. *Sources of Our Liberties*, Richard L. Perry, editor, New York: American Bar Foundation, 1952, pp. 264-265.

17. Samuel Adams, *The Writings of Samuel Adams*, Harry Alonzo Cushing, editor, New York: G.P. Putnam's Sons, 1908, vol. IV, p. 356, to the Legislature of Massachusetts on January 17, 1794.

18. John Jay, *The Life of John Jay*, William Jay, editor, New York: J. & J. Harper, 1833, Vol. II, p. 385, to John Murray on April 15, 1818.

19. James Wilson, *The Works of the Honourable James Wilson*, Bird Wilson, editor, Philadelphia: Lorenzo Press, 1804, Vol. I, p. 64, "Of the General Principles of Law and Obligation."

20. James Wilson, *Works*, Vol. 1, pp. 103-105, "Of the General Principles of Law and Obligation."

21. John Quincy Adams, *The Jubilee of the Constitution*, New York: Published by Samuel Colman, 1839, pp. 13-14.

22. Alexander Hamilton, *The Papers of Alexander Hamilton*, Harold Syrett, editor, NY: Columbia University Press, 1961, Vol. I, p. 87, from "The Farmer Refuted," February 23, 1775.

23. Noah Webster, *An American Dictionary of the English Language*, New York: S. Converse, 1828, definition of law, #3 and #6.

24. Rufus King, *The Life and Correspondence of Rufus King*, Charles R. King, editor, New York: G.P. Putnam's Sons, 1900, Vol. VI, p. 276, to C. Gore on February 17, 1820.

25. William Findley, Observations on "The Two Sons of Oil," Pittsburgh: Patterson and Hopkins, 1812, p. 35.

26. *The Federalist*, Edited by Michael Loyd Chadwick, Washington, D.C.: Global Affairs, p. 238.

27. *Writings of Thomas Jefferson*, ed. By Paul Leicester Ford, New York: G.P. Putnam's Sons, 1892-1899, Vol. I, p. 447.

28. In his original draft Jefferson wrote of man as created with certain inherent and inalienable rights. The drafting committee changed this to the present wording, which Jefferson embraced.

29. Zephaniah Swift, *A System of the Laws of the State of Connecticut*, Windham: John Byrne, 1795, Vol. I, pp. 6-7.

30. James Kent, *Commentaries on American Law*, seventh edition, New York: William Kent, 1851, p. 2, 4.

31. Andrew W. Young, *First Lessons in Civil Government,* Auburn, N.Y.: H. And J.C. Ivison, 1846, p. 16.

32. Thomas Paine, "Declaration of Rights," *The Writings of Thomas Paine*, Collected and edited by Daniel Conway, New York: G.P. Putnam's Sons, Vol. 3, p. 129-130.

33. Even Benjamin Franklin, who was not an orthodox Christian, said Paine's anti-Christian writings would only result in evil and should not be published (see *The Works of Benjamin Franklin*, Jared Sparks, editor. Boston: Tappan, Whittemore, and Mason, 1840, pp. 281-282.)

34. *For the Colony in Virginea Britannia, Lawes Divine, Morall and Martiall, etc.*, compiled by William Strachey, edited by David H. Flaherty, Charlottesville: University Press of Virginia, 1969, pp. 10-11.

35. *The Laws of the Pilgrims, A Facsimile Edition of The Book of the General Laws of the Inhabitants of the Jurisdiction of New-Plimouth, 1672 & 1685*, Wilmington, Del.: Pilgrim Society, 1977, p. 1.

36. *Sources of Our Liberties,* p. 148.

37. *The Blue Laws of New Haven Colony*, usually called Blue Laws of Connecticut . . . , By an antiquarian, Hartford: printed by Case, Tiffany & Co., 1838, p. 145.

38. *Sources of Our Liberties*, p. 216, 218, 220.

39. *Sources of Our Liberties*, p. 220.

40. *Sources of Our Liberties*, pp. 349, 350.

41. *Sources of Our Liberties,* pp. 373, 374.

42. *Sources of Our Liberties*, p. 382.

43. *The Constitutions of the Several Independent States of America*, Boston: Norman and Bowen, 1785, p. 146, South Carolina, 1776, Section 13.

44. *The Constitutions of the Sixteen States*, Boston: Manning and Loring, 1797, p. 274, Tennessee, 1796, Article VIII, Section II.

45. For a discussion of Christianity and the Constitution see Daniel L. Dreisbach, "In Search of a Christian Commonwealth: An Examination of Selected Nineteenth-Century Commentaries on References to God and the Christian Religion in the United States Constitution", *Baylor Law Review,* Fall 1996, Vol. 48, Number 4, pp. 928-1000. See also David Barton, *Original Intent*, Aledo, Tex.: WallBuilder Press, 1996.

46. *Sources of Our Liberties*, p. 396.

47. For more on the family see Stephen McDowell and Mark Beliles, *Liberating the Nations*, Charlottesville: Providence Foundation, 1995, chapter 8.

48. See Stephen McDowell, *Restoring America's Christian Education*, Charlottesville: Providence Foundation, 2000.

49. For an overview of Christian economics see Mark Beliles and Stephen McDowell, *America's Providential History*, Charlottesville: Providence Foundation, 1989, chapter 14.

50. See Alexis De Tocqueville, *Democracy in America*, Richard D. Heffner, editor, New York: The New American Library, 1963, pp. 198-202.

51. While all Americans were not Christians, almost all Americans had a Biblical worldview, even many nonbelievers. This was due to the central role the church played in the life of the nation, as well as to the fact that the educational institutions of this nation were Christian. Today, not only do the non-Christians not have a Biblical worldview, but even many Christians think like pagans (and in various areas, a majority of Christians have a humanistic worldview — it should be no surprise for nonbelievers to think and act like pagans, but when Christians think and act like the irreligious, we have a problem). They have a humanistic worldview because of the diminished influence of the church and the secularization of most of our educational, entertainment, and media institutions.

52. Morris, p. 239.

53. Morris, pp. 318-328.

54. From photocopies in our possession. Original printed copies of these sermons are in the WallBuilders library in Aledo, Texas.

55. From a photocopy of Henry's original will in our possession. See also, Moses Coit Tyler, *Patrick Henry*, Boston: Houghton, Mifflin, and Co., 1893, 145.

56. Will of Richard Stockton, May 20, 1780. In David Barton, *A Spiritual Heritage Tour of the United States Capitol*, Aledo, Tex.: WallBuilders, 2000, p. 28. This and the other Last Will and Testaments quoted in this book are from photocopies of original wills in our possession (courtesy of WallBuilders).

57. Last Will and Testament of Samuel Adams in David Barton, *The Practical Benefits of Christianity,* Aledo, Tex.: WallBuilder, 2001, 7-8.

58. Last Will and Testament of John Jay, in Barton, 7-8.

59. Last Will and Testament of George Mason, *The Life of George Mason*, Kate Mason Rowland, New York: G.P. Putnam's Sons, 1892, p. 457 (on CD Rom by WallBuilders, 2004).

60. Last Will and Testament of Robert Treat Paine, in Barton, 7-8.

61. Last Will and Testament of John Dickinson, in Barton, 7-8. For more exerpts from the wills of America's Founders see, "The Last Will & Testaments of the Founders Reveal Their Christian Faith," compiled by Stephen McDowell, *Providential Perspective*, Vol. 19, No. 4, August 2005, published by the Providence Foundation.

62. From an autographed letter written by Charles Carroll to Charles W. Wharton, Esq., on September 27, 1825, from Doughoragen, Maryland; possessed by WallBuilders.

63. Lewis Henry Boutell, *The Life of Roger Sherman,* Chicago: A.C. McClurg and Co., 1896, pp. 271-273.

64. Benjamin Rush, *The Autobiography of Benjamin Rush*, George Corner, ed., Princeton: University Press for the American Philosophical Society, 1948, p. 166.

65. E. Edwards Beardsley, *Life and Times of William Samuel Johnson, LL.D.*, Boston: Houghton, Mifflin, and Co., 1886, pp. 141-145, in Barton, *A Spiritual Heritage Tour of the United States Capitol*, pp. 61-62.

66. William B. Reed, *Life and Correspondence of Joseph Reed*, Philadelphia: Lindsay and Blakiston, 1847, pp. 36-37, in Barton, *A Spiritual Heritage Tour of the United States Capitol*, pp. 29-30.

67. Webster to Thomas Dawes, December 20, 1808. *Letters of Noah Webster*, Harry R. Warfel, editor, New York: Library Publishers, 1953, pp. 312-313.

68. Chauncey A. Goodrich, "Memoir of the Author," of *An American Dictionary of the English Language*, Philadelphia: J.B. Lippincott & Co., 1860, p. xxii.

69. See for example: Noah Webster, *An American Dictionary of the English Language*, "Memoir of the Author" by Chauncey A. Goodrich, editor, Philadelphia: J.B. Lippincott & Co., 1860, p. xxii.

70. For more on the power and form of our government see *Liberating the Nations* by McDowell and Beliles, chapters 1 and 11. For the Founders' views on this see, Stephen McDowell, *Building Godly Nations*, Charlottesville: Providence Foundation, 2004, Chapter 10, "We Hold These Truths — Governmental Principles of America's Founders.

71. *Church of the Holy Trinity v. U.S.*; 143 U.S. 457, 458 (1892).

72. *Updegraph v. The Commonwealth*; 11 Serg & R. 393, 394 (Sup. Ct. Penn. 1824).

73. *People v. Ruggles;* 8 Johns 545 (Sup. Ct. NY. 1811).

74. *Vidal v. Girard's Executors*; 8 Johns 545 (Sup. Ct. NY. 1811).

75. *Runkel v. Winemiller*; 4 Harris & McHenry 256, 259 (Sup. Ct. Md. 1799).

76. *City Council of Charleston v. S.A. Benjamin*; 2 Strob. 508, 518-520, 522-524 (Sup. Ct. S.C. 1846).

77. *Lindenmuller v. The People*, 33 Barb 548, (Sup. Ct. NY 1861).

78. *Shover v. State*; 10 English 259, 263 (Sup. Ct. Ark. 1850).

79. W. DeLoss Love, Jr., *The Fast and Thanksgiving Days of New England*, New York: Houghton, Mifflin and Co., 1895. For a few examples from Love's book see *America's Providential History, A Documentary Sourcebook,* Stephen

McDowell, editor, Charlottesville: Providence Foundation, 2004, chapter 8. See also *America's Providential History*, pp. 137, 141, 142, 163, 165, 176.

80. For more on these things see *America's Providential History*, chap. 10-12; and Stephen McDowell & Mark Beliles, *In God We Trust Tour Guide*, Charlottesville: Providence Foundation, 1998, pp. 26-27.

81. Letter of John Adams to Abigail, July 3d. 1776, *The Book of Abigail and John, Selected Letters of the Adams Family*, 1762-1784, Cambridge, Mass.: Harvard University Press, 1975, p. 142.

82. Alexis DeTocqueville, *Democracy in America*, Vol. 2, p. 152, in CD Sourcebook of American History, produced by Infobases, 1995.

83. Morris, pp. 318-328.

84. "A Letter to the Officers of the First Brigade of the Third Division of the Militia of Massachusetts, Oct. 11, 1798." In *The Works of John Adams, Second President of the United States*, Boston: Little, Brown and Co., 1854, 9:228-229.

85. Morris, p. 239.

86. George Washington, Letter to the Clergy of Different Denominations Residing in and near the City of Philadelphia, March 3, 1797, in *The Writings of George Washington*, Vol. 35, John C. Fitzpatrick, Editor, Washington: United States Government Printing Office, 1940, p. 416.

87. A Compilation of the *Messages and Papers of the Presidents,* By James D. Richardson, Washington: Bureau of National Literature and Art, 1910, 1:205-216.

88. James Madison, Letter to Frederick Beasley, Nov. 20, 1825.

89. James Madison, *Memorial and Remonstrance*, 1785, in Norman Cousins, *"In God We Trust," the Religious Beliefs and Ideas of the American Founding Fathers,* New York: Harper & Brothers, 1958, p. 301.

90. Noah Webster, *History of the United States*, New Haven: Durrie & Peck, 1833, p. v.

91. Benjamin Rush, *Essays, Literary, Moral and Philosophical*, Philadelphia: printed by Thomas and William Bradford, 1806, p. 93.

92. Jedidiah Morse, Election Sermon given at Charleston, MA on April 25, 1799.

93. *Sources of Our Liberties*, p. 382.

94. Bernard C. Steiner, *One Hundred and Ten Years of Bible Society Work in Maryland*, Baltimore: Maryland Bible Society, 1921, p. 14.

95. Samuel Adams, *The Writings of Samuel Adams*, Harry Alonzo Cushing, editor, New York: G.P. Putnam's Sons, 1905, Vol. IV, p. 74, to John Trumbull on October 16, 1778.

96. Bernard C. Steiner, *The Life and Correspondence of James McHenry*, Cleveland: The Burrows Brothers Company, 1907, p. 475, Charles Carroll to James McHenry on November 4, 1800.

97. Thomas Jefferson, *The Writings of Thomas Jefferson*, Albert Ellery Bergh, editor, Washington, D.C.: The Thomas Jefferson Memorial Association, 1904. Vol. XII, p. 315, to James Fishback, September 27, 1809.

98. Cited in Morris, p. 328.

99. *Ruggles* at 546.

100. Thomas Jefferson, *Memoir, Correspondence, and Miscellanies, From the Papers of Thomas Jefferson*, Thomas Jefferson Randolph, editor, Boston: Gray and Bowen, 1830, Vol. III, p. 509, to Benjamin Rush on April 21, 1803, Jefferson's "Syllabus of an Estimate of the Merit of the Doctrines of Jesus, Compared with Those of Others."

101. Baron De Montesquieu, *The Spirit of Laws*, translated from the French by Thomas Nugent, 2 Vols., New York: the Colonial Press, 1899, Vol. 2, p. 27.

102. Ibid., pp. 29, 30.

103. McCormick also developed the business of making and selling reapers. See *Building Godly Nations*, chapter 14.

104. *Building Godly Nations*, pp. 7-9.

105. *Building Godly Nations*, pp. 9-12.

106. For more on the central role of the Bible see *Building Godly Nations*, chapter 4.

107. Noah Webster, *History of the United States*, New Haven: Durrie & Peck, 1833, pp. 273-274.

108. See *America's Providential History*, pp. 248 ff.

109. Morris, p. 270.

About the Providence Foundation

The Providence Foundation is a Christian educational organization whose mission is to train and network leaders to transform their culture for Christ, and to teach all citizens how to disciple nations. We have been working since our inception in 1983 to fulfill Christ's commission to "make disciples of all nations." Such nations will have transformed people, but also transformed institutions — family, church, and state.

The Foundation has focused on training and networking leaders in a principled, Biblical education that has historically produced liberty, justice, prosperity, virtue, and knowledge in people and nations. The Providence Foundation advances its mission through:

Biblical Worldview University

Multi-national Church-based Discipleship of Leaders in Schools, Media, Business and Politics • President: Stephen McDowell

How we can serve you:

- Books, videos, audios, correspondence courses, and online classes
- Live worldview training seminars in cities throughout America and numerous nations
- *Providential Perspective* Newsletter – a regular educational journal for members
- In God We Trust Christian history tours to see America's landmarks of liberty

We invite you to enroll in our courses, host a seminar or class in your area, or become one of our instructors. Contact us or go to www.worldviewuniversity.com for more information.

National Transformation Network

Multi-national Church-based Mentoring and Teamwork of Leaders in Schools, Media, Business & Politics • President: Dr. Mark Beliles

How we can serve you:

- Monthly emailed newsletter for leadership teams in each sphere of influence
- Transformation Project summits to help leaders to develop strategic plans in their cities

- Online video conferencing, web-forums and networking of leadership teams by sphere & region
- Special networking of pastors via our U.S. Pastor Council

Join online, host a summit in your area, or become one of our Transformation Team mentors in your area. Contact us or go to www.nationaltransformation.com for more information.

Help us in Transforming Nations:

- Become a MEMBER of the Providence Foundation by donating at least $100/year (or $10/month) and receive our educational newsletter and discounts on products and seminar fees.
- Become a PREMIUM MEMBER: those who contribute $300 or more per year receive Member benefits plus a free book, $80 voucher toward one of our BWU Courses, personal coaching, and more.
- To receive our free e-newsletter send your email to info@ providencefoundation.com

For more information contact: Providence Foundation, PO Box 6759, Charlottesville, VA 22906, 434-978-4535, providencefoundation.com, Email: info@providencefoundation.com

Biblical Worldview University

Training leaders of education, business, and politics to transform their culture for Christ.

The Biblical Worldview University (BWU) provides training for leaders of all ages and spheres of life in a curriculum of real-world topics, offered via distance learning (on DVD, CDs, and/or print) and eventually on-line in multiple languages. Live classes are also offered throughout the year at study centers in Charlottesville, Virginia, and in other parts of the world.

BWU seeks to train those who equip others, so graduates of the school may become Providence Foundation Instructors or Facilitators who teach or lead others in Biblical worldview courses. BWU offers dozens of courses under five general areas of study (some courses are listed below). Start your Biblical worldview training today by ordering one or more of the following courses. To enroll for credit ask for an enrollment form. Contact us for a course catalog or visit our website.

General Biblical Worldview

1. Fundamentals for Biblical Transformation — [Cost: $80; Audit: $50; 8 hrs.; BWV01]

2. Providential World History: The Chain of Liberty — [$110; Audit: $80; 11 hrs.; BWV02]

3. Must the Sun Set on the West? — [Cost: $80; Audit: $50; 10 hrs.; BWV03]

Providential History

1. Foundations of a Biblical Worldview and Providential History — [$130; Audit: $100; 11 hrs.; HIS01]

2. America's Christian History (Vision and Planting)—[$110; Audit: $80; 10 hrs.; HIS02]

3. America's Christian History (Beginning and Growth) — [$110; Audit: $80; 10 hrs.; HIS03]

4. The American Heritage Series — [$120; Audit: $90; 10 hours; HIS04]

5. America's Providential History — [Cost: $100; Audit: $50; 22 hrs.; HIS05]

6. Revival — [Cost: $45; Audit: $25; 4 hrs.; HIS06]

7. America, a Christian Nation? Examining the Evidence of the Christian Foundation of America — [Cost: $40; Audit: $20; 3 hrs.; HIS08]

8. Apostle of Liberty: the World-Changing Leadership of George Washington — [Cost: $55; Audit: $35; 5 hrs.; HIS10]

9. Churches and Politics in Jefferson's Virginia — [Cost: $40; Audit: $15; 4 hrs.; HIS11]

The Family and Christian Education

1. Christian Education & Biblical Worldview — [Cost: $120; Audit: $90; 8 hrs.; EDU 01]

2. The Principle Approach to Education for Home or Church Schools — [Cost: $200; Audit: $160; 20 hrs.; EDU02]

3. A Guide to American Christian Education for the Home & School: The Principle Approach — [Cost: $80; Audit: $50; 16 hrs.; EDU03]

4. God's Health Plan — [Cost: $55; Audit: $35; 5 hrs.; EDU04]

The Marketplace — Business, Economics, and Finance

1. Foundations of Biblical Economics, Business and the Marketplace — [Cost: $70; Audit: $45; 5 hrs.; MKT01]

2. Economics from a Christian Perspective — [Cost: $50; Audit: $30; 3 hrs.; MKT02]

3. Biblical Economics and Personal Finance — [Cost: $130; Audit: $100; 15 hrs.; MKT03]

The State — Government, Law, and Political Science

1. God & Government —[Cost: $70; Audit: $40; 6 hrs.; STA01]

2. Discipling the Nations — [Cost: $70; Audit: $40; 4 hrs.; STA02]

3. Biblical Law and Social Action — [Cost: $120; Audit: $90; 9 hrs.; STA03]

4. Government and Politics — [Cost: $110; Audit: $80; 9 hrs.; STA04]

5. Family Policy Perspectives — [Cost: $70; Audit: $40; 5 hrs.; STA05]

6. Building Godly Nations — [Cost: $110; Audit: $80; 12 hrs.; STA06]

7. Liberating the Nations — [Cost: $50; Audit: $20; 5 hrs.; STA05]

8. The Declaration of Independence — [Cost: $50; Audit: $20; 5 hrs.; STA07]

9. The Bible and the Constitution — [Cost: $80; Audit: $50; 5 hrs.; STA08]

10. The Constitution of the United States — [Cost: $50; Audit: $20; 5 hrs.; STA09]

11. Jefferson's "Wall of Separation of Church and State" — [$80; Audit: $50; 6 hrs.; STA10]

12. Running God's Way: Step By Step to a Successful Political Campaign — [Cost: $45; Audit: $25; 4 hrs.; STA11]

Providence Foundation Resources

Books

America's Providential History   (B01) $18.95
> How the Lord guided our nation from the very beginning. Proof from history: our nation grew from Christian principles. How to bring them back into the mainstream.

America's Providential History Documentary Sourcebook   (B16) $17.95

America's Providential History Teacher's Guide   (B17) $16.95

Liberating the Nations   (B02) $15.95
> God's plan, fundamental principles, essential foundations, and structures necessary to build Christian nations.

Defending the Declaration   (B04) $15.95
> How the Bible and Christianity influenced the writing of the Declaration.

Watchmen on the Walls   (B06) $8.95
> The role of pastors in equipping Christians to fulfill their civil duties.

In God We Trust   (B03) $15.95
> A Christian tour guide for historic sites in D.C., Philadelphia, & Virginia.

Apostle of Liberty   (B20) $16.95
> The World-Changing Leadership of George Washington. A brief bio of the father of America from a providential perspective.

Building Godly Nations   (B14) $16.95
> The mandate for building Godly nations, lessons from America's Christian history, and how to apply Biblical principles to governing the nations.

Contending for the Constitution   (B15) $15.95
> Recalling the Christian influence on the writing of the Constitution and the Biblical basis of American law and liberty.

America, a Christian Nation?   (B18) $8.95
> Examining the evidence of the Christian foundation of America.

In Search of Democracy   (B07) $6.95
> Foundations, framework, and historical development of biblical government and law.

Independence, Drums of War, vol. 1   (B08) $8.95

Bunker Hill, Drums of War, vol. 2   (B09) $8.95

A Captive in Williamsburg, Drums of War, vol. 3   (B10) $8.95
> Drums of War is a series of historical novels for young people designed to teach in an enjoyable way the principles, events, and persons behind America's independence.

The Ten Commandments and Modern Society   (B11) $5.95

Restoring America's Christian Education   (B12) $5.95

A Guide to American Christian Education   (B13) $39.95
> Hardback book on the Principle Approach to Education.

Rendering to Caesar the Things That Are God's   (PP01) $4.95

The American Dream: Jamestown and the Planting of America   (B19) $11.95

DVDs (Videos)

The Story of America's Liberty   (DVD01 or VT01) $19.95
> A 60-minute video that looks at the influence of Christianity in the beginning of America, examining principles and providential occurrences.

Dawn's Early Light   (DVD02 or VT02) $19.95
> A 28-minute version of *The Story of America's Liberty* with up-dated statistics.

The Wall   (DVD03 or VT03) $19.95

Documentary on the historical roots of "the wall of separation" metaphor.

Stand Up & Be Counted   (DVD04) $19.95

Three TV programs by Joyce Meyer Ministries on our reponsibilities as Americans to maintain our liberties. With Joyce and Dave Meyer, Alan Keyes, Peter Marshall, Stephen McDowell, and Mark Beliles.

A Nation Adrift   (DVD05 or VT05) $19.95

CDs and Audiotapes

America's Freedom: Founded on Faith (AT15)(CD15)	$5.95
No Cross, No Crown: Exemplified in the Life of William Penn (AT1) (CD1)	$5.95
Reforming the Nations—an Example from the Life of Webster (AT2) (CD2)	$5.95
Teaching History from a Providential Perspective (AT10)(CD10)	$5.95
The Principle Approach (AT9) (CD9)	$5.95
The Principle Approach: Teaching History & Literature (AT19) (CD19)	$5.95
God Governs in the Affairs of Men (AT11)(CD11)	$5.95
Biblical Economics (AT7) (CD7)	$5.95
Honest Money and Banking (AT8) (CD8)	$5.95
Biblical Government and Law (AT5) (CD5)	$5.95
Forming a Christian Union (AT6) (CD6)	$5.95
Role of Women in History (AT13) (CD13)	$5.95
Fundamental Principles of Christian Nations (AT3)(CD3)	$5.95
Christ's Teaching on Public Affairs (AT4)(CD4)	$5.95
Biblical Principles of Business, Exemplified by McCormick (AT16) (CD16)	$5.95
We Hold These Truths—Governmental Principles of Founders (AT12) (CD12)	$5.95
American Christian Revolution (AT14) (CD14)	$5.95
Education and the Kingdom of God (AT17) (CD17)	$5.95
Biblical Relationship of Church & State (AT18) (CD18)	$5.95
Prophetic Christian Statesmanship (AT20)	$5.95
Ten Commandments & Modern Society (AT21) (CD21)	$5.95
Why We Celebrate Thanksgiving (AT27) (CD27)	$5.95
Qualifications for Godly Officials (AT26) (CD26)	$5.95
Thomas Jefferson on "The Foundation of America's Liberty" (AT28) (CD28)	$5.95
Jesus: the Focal Point of History (AT25) (CD25)	$5.95
Loving God with All Your Mind (AT24) (CD24)	$5.95
Fulfilling the Cultural Mandate: How Christians Have Helped Establish God's Kingdom in the Nations (AT23) (CD23	$5.95
Christ the King (AT22) (CD22)	$5.95
The Hand of Providence (AT31) (CD31)	$5.95
Fast & Thanksgiving Days in Early America (AT29) (CD29)	$5.95
Marcus & Narcissa Whitman and the Cultural Mandate (AT30) (CD30)	$5.95
Richard Hakluyt & the Providential Colonization of America (AT38) (CD38)	$5.95
The Christian Influence in Jamestown and Early Virginia (AT32) (CD32)	$5.95
Lister and Biblical Medical Principles (AT35) (CD35)	$5.95
Crime and Punishment (AT34) (CD34)	$5.95
Economy from a Biblical Perspective (AT33) (CD33)	$5.95
Separation of Church and State (AT39) (CD39)	$5.95

RESPONSE & ORDER FORM

I want to join the Providence Foundation by becoming a:

☐ **MEMBER**: those who contribute $100 or more per year receive our newsletters, a 30% discount on all our books, videos, and materials, plus discounts to our Seminars. I will send a regular gift of $_____ per month / quarter / year (circle one). Enclosed is my gift of: | $

☐ **PREMIUM MEMBER**: those who contribute $300 or more per year receive Member benefits plus a free book, $80 voucher toward one of our BWU Courses, & personal coaching. I will send a regular gift of $_____ per month/quarter/year (circle one). Enclosed is my gift of: | $

☐ **SUPPORTER**: those who contribute $25 or more receive the *Providential Perspective* and *Reformation Report*. Enclosed is my gift of: | $

I wish to order the following items:

Qty	Title/Product code		Price	Total

	Subtotal	
Shipping & Handling :	Member disct. (30%)	
* U.S. Mail: $4.00 minimum, 10% if over $35	Sales tax (VA orders add 5%)	
* UPS: $5.50 minimum, 12% if over $50.	**Shipping**	
(Game orders will be sent UPS)	**TOTAL**	
	Contribution	
☐ Please send me a Resource Catalog	**GRAND TOTAL**	

Method of Payment: ☐ Check/M.O.   ☐ VISA   ☐ MC   ☐ AmEx   ☐ Cash

Credit Card No.:_____ Exp. date: _____

Signature:_____

SHIP TO:

Name:_____

Address:_____

City:_____ State:_____ Zip:_____

Phone:(_____)_____

Email:_____

Make checks payable to:
Providence Foundation
PO Box 6759
Charlottesville, VA 22906
Phone: 434-978-4535

Also, order by phone or at website
www.providencefoundation.com